In
Defense
of
Truth

Timothy M. Duffy

ISBN 1-59196-099-1

First Printing, August 2002

For additional copies of this book,
please write to:

Timothy Duffy
3762 West Old 30, Lot 55E
Warsaw, IN 46580
Or visit our website: http://members.kconline.com/dot

Please enclose $5.00 per book
(this <u>includes</u> postage and packaging)
Make checks or money orders payable to Tim Duffy.

Acknowledgments:

I want to thank my sister, Sondra, for reading the manuscript and giving many helpful hints. Most of all, I want to thank my bride, Brenda, for enduring many nights of listening to me read parts of the book, and her own readings and suggestions that helped make this project possible. And Anna, thank you for letting daddy work while you patiently watched.

Contents

Part 1
The Spirit of Truth and The Spirit of Error

"We are of God: he that knoweth God heareth us; he that is not of God heareth not us. Hereby know we the spirit of truth, and the spirit of error."

1 John 4:6

Chapter 1
Priorities in Dangerous Times

"This know also, that in the last days perilous times shall come. For men shall be lovers of their own selves, covetous, boasters, proud, blasphemers, disobedient to parents, unthankful, unholy, Without natural affection, trucebreakers, false accusers, incontinent, fierce, despisers of those that are good, Traitors, heady, highminded, lovers of pleasures more than lovers of God; Having a form of godliness, but denying the power thereof: from such turn away" (2 Timothy 3:1-5).

"But evil men and seducers shall wax worse and worse, deceiving, and being deceived" (2 Timothy 3:13).

Paul's predictions, by the Holy Ghost, are happening today. This list of ungodly lifestyles surrounds us right now. Look at it again.

These last days, before the catching away of the church, are a time of great deception. "Winds of doctrine" have fooled many, who once had a revelation of Jesus Christ, into believing another gospel. Perilous (dangerous) times are here.

Dangerous times force us to act differently. We must stay alert, not becoming intoxicated with the world's excesses or we will fail to notice deceiving spirits. Our tendency is to loose spiritual hearing and eyesight when we become "full." Prosperity can deceive us into thinking we brought it to ourselves, leaving a feeling of power and then ease. Beware; comfortable people get into spiritual trouble.

We will pay a heavy price for not staying alert. Those who do not pay attention will drift into false doctrine by believing a lie and being damned.

The Priority of Sound Doctrine in Evangelism

As the church completes its time on earth, sound doctrine is top priority – nothing else is more important. Do not let any person or devil fool you into minimizing or letting up on the Apostle's Doctrine.

Satan wants us to back off sound teaching and move into the people pleasing business, so the wishes of individuals will determine what we preach. He wants us to buy into his lie that people feel uncomfortable with our gospel message, tempting us to alter or hide elements of the gospel that require change.

Jesus said the world would hate those who believe in and follow Him, because the Light of the gospel reveals sin and requires repentance (John 15:18-22). The gospel may make some people our enemy because we preach they need to stop living a sinful lifestyle.

Often, many churches do not promote the preaching of repentance, baptism in water in the name of Jesus Christ for the remission of sins and receiving the Holy Ghost, speaking in tongues, because it may not "go over" well with the crowd.

The devil has slipped in the belief that people are not interested in our doctrine, only our acceptance of them the way they are. He knows if we treat people like customers, they will determine what we preach. After all, remember the old saying, "The customer is always right."

We must remember that the church is not a customer/

8

salesman-based entity. It is a body – a living organism of people placed together by God through a new birth into a new family – God's family. The church is not a business in the sense of earthly corporations.

Satan wants to trick us into becoming concerned with people's acceptance of what we preach and teach. He wants the basis or foundation of "membership" in the local church to be based on social acceptance. This will lead to the eventual abandonment of the true message. It will become a message of convenience for them and us.

If you have offended someone in the past by preaching the Apostle's Doctrine, do not feel intimidated or feel forced to move the message to a more "convenient time," because you will not find one.

The best time to reveal the apostolic message is right away. It makes no sense to hide their lost condition from them. Why wait weeks or months to find a place to insert the teaching that will save their soul? What would happen if Jesus came back for the church while we wait?

If pleasing people is our priority, we will become promoters of ways to make them feel better. On the other hand, if seeing people turn from sin to walk with Jesus is our priority, we will be promoters of preaching the gospel to every person we meet right away.

Be careful not to cover up the true message until you think it is convenient. It may never be convenient. The great danger is changing the gospel to meet the expectations of those that hear us.

"I marvel that ye are so soon removed from him that called you into the grace of Christ unto another gospel: Which is not another; but there be some that trouble you, and would pervert the gospel of Christ. But though we, or an angel from heaven, preach any other gospel unto you than that which we have preached unto you, let him be accursed" (Galatians 1:6-8).

Chapter 2
We Must Sound the Warning

Today, Satan's standards for living are replacing godly principles, sinful lifestyles are encouraged to exist through tolerance, and as a result, there is a loss of the revelation of Jesus Christ to man-made ideas of an "unknowable" God. All of this is pressing in on the church; therefore, we must sound the alarm.

Proper warnings can be rare because deceivers say, "Warnings are negative and people won't come to Jesus Christ or stay with our church if we make negative statements."

Being wrong always brings a negative feeling. The truth about humanity's sin-nature is painful to hear, especially if you think you are okay the way you are. Nevertheless, it is time to give and hear warnings about sinful lives, false doctrines, and false prophets. It is time to talk about seducing spirits and their doctrines of damnation.

Being negative is not the issue when it is God's Word. God is negative on sin and always will be, so we must declare it. Teachers of man's wisdom are the ones who have tried to convince us to never saying anything negative, not God. God desires a change from sin to obedience. The only way to see change in the lives of people is to preach full responsibility for their actions. We must tell people to repent of their sins, which is a change of mind and change of direction in life.

It is time to own up to our responsibility to God and His church. To be in the true church we must (1) find the truth, (2) do the truth, and (3) preach the truth.

Jesus Christ warned, "Beware of false prophets…"(Matthew 7:15). This is a negative statement, but if we listen, it will save our souls from the deception of Satan. Do not judge something as truth based on whether it is negative in nature. If you use this as a criterion, you will miss many things Jesus is saying to you.

The very nature of the Law of God is negative because it reveals what is wrong with the human race. We are all proven sinners by God's Law. This will not leave us with a positive feeling. This is God's design – He wants to bring conviction. God does not want people to feel good about their sinful lives. He is Light and it reveals who we really are – sinners. The original apostolic gospel, when preached, reveals all sin and gives a remedy of complete deliverance.

The gospel (good news) of Jesus Christ is His death, burial, and resurrection. His death and burial is the negative parts that are necessary for the positive part. Deliverance from sin by the power of the resurrection is the positive part of the gospel, but we first must die to the lusts of our flesh and eyes and deny the pride of life that rebels against the will of God. Being baptized in the name of Jesus Christ is burying our old sinful nature into the death of Jesus. Now, the positive power of the resurrection (Holy Ghost) can be a reality in our lives.

Those deceived by the Positive Mental Attitude crowd consider it wrong to speak of man's gross sins. However, the Light of God is the only way to reveal sin and produce a turning to Him. A change of mind that produces a change of lifestyle is true repentance. The spoken Word of God is the only Word that generates the need for repentance in the hearer. This is the painful part required to bring the power and glory of a new life.

Double-check your gospel if people do not have a change of life or do not feel they need to be different. If we learn to cope with our own sins and teach tolerance of other sinful lifestyles, we are listening to the wrong voice.

Human philosophy has deceived many into believing lifestyles do not have to be free of repetitive sin. Some claim we should not say, "Do not do that," because it is an infringement on personal convictions. We had better take a closer look at "personal convictions" and see if it is not a device of the devil to place leadership in a neutral position. Is Satan tempting us to leave people alone? We had better make sure he is not trying to silence the voice of truth.

Satan loves to fool us into thinking we can stay neutral on any subject and thus be a "friend" to everyone. He says, "Let the individual pick what is right for them and just be their friend."

This is a trick with deadly consequences. With this so-called freedom in neutrality, no one warns them of the first steps away from God into a lifestyle of unbelief and eventual spiritual collapse. They may never see it because no one will tell them; after all, they have a right to do what they want – they have their personal convictions to guide them.

If people know what is best for them, any outside authority must become neutral to accommodate each system of belief. Actually, this neutrality destroys any authority for their lives, except their own.

Fear then becomes the method of governing because we dare not trample on the personal convictions of another person in the church. Fear stops people from speaking out against sin. Some local churches live by this standard of fear, which is creating tolerance of sin. If we tolerate sin long enough, we will soon participate.

In this system, everyone is right in his own eyes. If everyone is right, then nobody is wrong, and to say people are wrong brings defense of their territory – each person is their own king with their own kingdom of beliefs. "Do not mess with what I believe," becomes the battle cry.

If we only rely on what each individual thinks is best for them, then there are no universal sins to preach against any more. This is Satan's way of silencing the messenger from declaring the Law of God. This will cause the local church to fracture into segregated pools of thinking, producing political factions striving to please each viewpoint.

Leading people is not about seeking their acceptance. Leadership is as much about confronting, warnings of error, and stopping forward movement as it is about directing where to go. Sometimes we need to stop, back up, and allow a holy detour. It's all about obedience to the Head of the church – Jesus Christ.

If we fear what man thinks, we cannot lead God's way, nor will we confront sin. Without confrontation, sin no longer will be an issue until it is too late. It is too late when we deal with the consequences of our silence.

Not all confrontations have to end in shouting matches if we learn to confront with compassions, humility and godly timing. The key here is to follow the leading of the Spirit.

Confrontations can be intimidating, so they are often abandoned for read-between-the-lines suggestions, hoping the hearer will take the hint. This approach does not help people grow into mature Christians. It just teaches them to take hints and avoid resolutions to their problems.

People that want to live right will respond in the right attitude to someone they know cares enough to address them directly. If they do not change, they at least cannot ask later why we did not warn them. Furthermore, the devil is the one that has promoted the lie that warnings or saying no to sin drives people away.

All godly leadership will sound an alarm from time to time as God reveals what is ahead for His church and the individuals in it. God will always show leaders what is ahead. He does not give every detail, but does give the general direction and how to proceed. He will fill obedient leadership with wisdom and instruction.

Aimless leadership is dangerous – someone must show the way. Jesus is not aimless and neither are His disciples. If we do not have the vision of what will happen in the future based on current behaviors and trends in the local church, then we are missing a most important ingredient of leadership. Watch out for deception to be present. This type of leader leads by how he feels or what people think of him this week, not by what God has directed him to do. Fear of the people's rejection will cancel the needed warnings for those who are moving toward error.

Carefully look at the following caution by the Apostle Paul, "Take heed therefore unto yourselves, and to all the flock, over the which the Holy Ghost hath made you overseers, to feed the church of God, which he hath purchased with his own blood. For I know this, that after my departing shall grievous wolves enter in among you, not sparing the flock. Also of your own selves shall men arise, speaking perverse things, to draw away disciples after them. Therefore watch, and remember, that by the space of three years I ceased not to warn every one night and day with tears" (Acts 20:28-31).

The entire church must work together to stay vigilant. If no one ever hears a warning about false teachings, this indicates the spirit of error in our midst. Satan doesn't want the congregation to be alert. So, he doesn't want us looking for false prophets or their teachings.

On the other hand, a pastor or leader may feel like warning the congregation of the spirit of error, but sense pressure from the people to back off. Feeling pressure is not always an indication to close up our Bibles, and pray "get me out of this one God," or give up and dismiss early.

Resistance from a congregation should propell us to teach more on the subject that brought the resistance. Investigate why the people are pushing back in their spirits and ask God to give the needed discernment and wisdom to root out and throw away these false strongholds.

Whenever a teacher or preacher makes a stand against sin, irrational behavior is often seen. It's like discovering a secret closet. The closer you get to the door the more heated the attempt to distract you. And, if you ever get your hand on the door knob, the behavior may move from irrational to rediculous.

These doors must be jerked open by the power and demonstration of the Spirit of God. Not with man's methods, but with the Light of apostolic authority over every false way in the name of Jesus Christ.

Chapter 3
The Use of Repetition

Some say, "People are bored with the same old teaching over and over," or, "You need to keep up with the times – spice it up." These ideas are forcing many people to look for a way to add some zing to the message and make it more palatable to the public. Some are even looking for ways to change it for the modern era.

It is sad when we think we have to apologize for repeating this same gospel message for centuries. God's plan is to have a church that preaches the same gospel repeatedly until every person in the world has heard it. This gospel message is a miracle producing Word that has worked for approximately 2000 years. Just do it, do not explain it away in the context of modern philosophy and man-made wisdom. After you preach the truth of the Word, you will greatly admire its power in the many changed lives.

We need to preach the simple gospel of Jesus Christ repeatedly. If we stick with what we already know is true, we would see the power of it. We do not have to "jazz" up the gospel or modify it to match new religious thoughts and trends of religious society.

Just because you preach something once with no apparent result does not mean it was ineffective or is not worth repeating. Repeat the truth and see what happens over time. Furthermore, we already know many will reject the true apostolic message, tempting us quite. Nevertheless, we must continue until we have told every person we meet.

If we preach repentance of a sinful lifestyle and baptism by immersion in water in the name of Jesus Christ for the remission of sins, those who believe it will do it. Many give up too quickly because it did not work, or appeared not to work, the first time.

Some churches have just left behind the elementary principle of *good* repetition. The Apostles practiced this and it brought the demonstration of the Spirit of God. Trouble comes to our churches when we forget this basic principle and move to some new thing "floating" around.

If we retreat, it comes from the badgering we get from the devil convincing us to "lighten up" and appeal to people's carnal desires. "Lightening up" does not necessarily appeal to more people, it just appeals to a different kind of people. Change the gospel and you will fill a congregation with rebellion.

The father of false doctrine, Satan, is the father of iniquity (rebellion against God). He teaches the world how to rebel against the voice of God by enlisting mouthpieces to carry the deception – false prophets and teachers.

Evil men and seducers are not going away until Jesus comes to the earth with thousands and thousands of His saints. Paul predicted, by the Holy Ghost, these types of men were going to increase in their evil and seduction. The only way for the church to overcome this growing seduction is to recognize the spirit of error and expel it.

Bad Repetition

On the other hand, man-made repetitive teachings are harmful because they promote man's thinking into the church.

For example, programmed services with no latitude for God's intervention have become common in some churches. This repetition is harmful because God has no "room" to move – He is in a "box." These types of assemblages have no eternal value. True value comes only when God speaks through leadership and members of the church for the profit of the whole body.

Each gathering of people presents a unique set of needs for the working of the Spirit of God. The gifts of the Spirit are an important part of bringing God's Word to us. We must hear from God. Without hearing, we do not know how to live right.

What is the church supposed to be? When we gather together each week for our services, what are we accomplishing? Do we do the same rituals every week? If so, this is the way of error – carnal repetitions of the spiritually dead.

Coming together every week and doing the same routine, all within the same time frame is not of God. We have put a "fence" around God by limiting Him to a certain amount of time for our assembling together. If we say our church services have to be over at a certain time you can be sure you will miss what God wants to do.

We must stop the spirit of error that pressures us to program every aspect of corporate gatherings. We might be surprized at how well organized a service would be if left up to the direction of the Holy Ghost. Just because we fail along the way to see Holy organization is no reason to abandon the learning curve of moving with the Spirit.

The gathering of the body of Christ is ultimately to worship God and hear from Him, which edifies the Body and promotes evangelism. It's a time for God to confirm what He has spoken to each individual or family unit. We must never leave a gathering without hearing from God or it is pointless.

"How is it then, brethren? when ye come together, every one of you hath a psalm, hath a doctrine, hath a tongue, hath a revelation, hath an interpretation. Let all things be done unto edifying" (1 Corinthians 14:26).

How do you feel when you leave a gathering of your brothers and sisters in the Lord? What has been accomplished when we part company?

There is a growing trend among us to use our gathering together as a church body for performances. Choirs are not for entertainment and singing groups are not professional concert performers. We frequently are more concerned about getting every note right instead of getting our hearts right. We practice and practice every part of the performance until we are like professional performers that get literal applause from an audience.

A man-made religious performance is easy to accomplish because it appeals to fleshly desires. Doing and teaching truth, along with truly worshipping God requires full responsibility and commitment of our minds and hearts. Not only that, but it requires intervention of a supernatural God in our lives. This requires a death to self and submission to the Lord. Otherwise, we will start to perform worthless rituals when we come together as a church body. This does not produce spiritual families and churches.

The church service should not be like going to a theater. Think about it, actors in the church showing us a pretend or real event. This usually promotes an emotional response that goes away when we leave the performance. Little by little, we have allowed Broadway and Hollywood to influence our gatherings. This, for some, has become the acceptable standard. We do not need to waste time performing for each other, while we have whole cities needing to hear a preacher.

> "How then shall they call on him in whom they have not believed? and how shall they believe in him of whom they have not heard? and how shall they hear without a preacher?" (Romans 10:14)

We can put so much pressure on ourselves to have a worldly standard of quality to our services that we miss the moving of the Spirit. If we miss the moving of God very often, you can be sure that false doctrine will come.

The enemy wants to stop the preacher; and if he does, faith in Jesus Christ dies.

Chapter 4
Methods of Deception

Satan is 100% deception and his design is to destroy our obedience to the Word of God. Here are four methods he is using to bring deception today.

Information Flood Method

It is staggering, the amount of information we have at our fingertips. When information comes at blinding speeds and large quantities, we ignore a great deal of it because we are not able to digest it. This begins one of the building blocks used for deception.

In a church setting, we also have much to digest. We have church libraries and stores filled with books and magazines, sermon tapes, gospel music tapes, cds, and videos. We have enough to keep us busy watching, listening, and reading for the rest of our lives. This is in addition to all the secular information we ingest.

How can we possibly digest all that is available to pastors and the members of our churches? This question can put us in a precarious spot. Do we ignore those things we cannot check out for their doctrinal soundness and allow them to be available? Can we ignore the possibility of evil influences?

If our conclusion is to ignore the possibility of false doctrine, we are moving into the trap. The answer is to be careful of surrounding ourselves with more than we actually need. Careful and prayerful inventory would reveal the need to lighten the load of information into our minds.

We must all be careful of what we read, view, and listen to from day to day. We must be fully aware of the kind of information allowed to run through our minds. The increased volume of material is a tool of deception. Do not allow the abundance of information to introduce you and your family to false doctrine. It can happen before you notice.

The Forked Tongue Method

The Forked Tongue method is speaking lies and truth together. Satan is the father of this method.

If we consume information by people that do not believe the Apostle's Doctrine and then take their teachings as truth, we are opening ourselves for trouble. This also includes listening to "Christian" music. We may think we are expert sorters of truth from error. Is it possible to continually put error into our minds, even in small portions, without it adversely effecting us?

Remember, Satan is not afraid of using the Word of God as long as he can mix it with false doctrine. He has done this from the beginning of humanity with his deception of Eve and will continue to do so. He loves using the Word of God mixed with lies. He knows many people are not aware of this method of deception, so he baits them and then switches to false doctrine. He will speak enough truth to relax you, and then slip in a false statement.

When we read or hear a questionable statement, we may say, "Hey, wait a minute, what was that again? I need to check that out." Before you have enough time to research it, he begins speaking more truth to keep you quiet, relaxed, and disregarding the lie. We may think there is some truth in what was stated, but this is Satan attempting to push lies into your mind. Partial truth should set off an alarm in our minds. Satan wants us to become accustomed to permitting error to flow through our minds un-challenged, until we become accustomed to hearing them.

When you hear something repeatedly and never challenge it with the Word of God, you will begin to believe it as the truth. We allow many lies to go unchecked because they are sand-wiched in truth or come from someone we trust is telling us the truth.

We must be careful not to allow the presence of occasional truth to fool us into believing all we hear.

The idea is to slowly remove truth and leave the false. It is a slow shift so it does not get our attention. Beware; a little yeast affects the whole lump of dough.

As an example, you may be reading a book someone recom-mended to you, and as you read, you notice some statements of false doctrine. You also notice it has many good things in it so you tell yourself you know truth from error, so you read on.

This process repeats, book after book, article after article, and tape after tape, until the false doctrinal phrases begin to etch their error into your mind. Before long, you will be thinking wrong and then speaking error. Truth and error begins to blend until we become confused, and confusion is the beginning of de-ception.

Confusion stops when the Word of God revealed by the Holy Ghost becomes our source for life. The Word of God must be the sole authority of the church.

Bypassing Authority Method

"And the LORD God commanded the man, saying, Of every tree of the garden thou mayest freely eat: But of the tree of the knowledge of good and evil, thou shalt not eat of it: for in the day that thou eatest thereof thou shalt surely die" (Genesis 2:16,17).

God gave Adam some very important instructions. He told him he could freely eat of every tree except the tree of knowl-edge of good and evil.

Adam was the first to receive the instruction from God, not Eve. God gave these instructions to Adam before he created the woman. This is the design of God—the man is the leader of the family. The husband is responsible to instruct everyone in the family unit of God's commandments. The wife/mother is not responsible for giving direction concerning God's commandments to her head (husband).

Satan knew God gave these instructions to Adam alone, thus making Eve the most vulnerable to his deception. He also knew the power of hearing God's voice directly; therefore, he did not direct his deceptive communication to Adam.

We know Adam had passed on the information about the tree of the knowledge of good and evil because of Eve's response to the serpent when asked about God's commandment. Eve said, "God hath said, Ye shall not eat of it, neither shall ye touch it, lest ye die." She knew what God's commandment was concerning the tree.

The serpent did not say, "Hey Eve, go get your husband and have him tell you what God said again." No, he immediately jumped over her God-given authority and said, "Yea, hath God said, Ye shall not eat of every tree of the garden?" Satan first attacked the most vulnerable person convincing her to question and discount the Word of God transferred to them by their God-given authority — Adam.

Eve then became the persuader of Adam to sin (disobey God's Word) because she found a "better way." She, through deception, disrupted the design of the family, which is the husband being the head of the wife and the wife being in submission to her husband. When Lucifer was finished with her, he convinced her to become the head or leader of Adam. This threw the first family into a state where Satan works best – the wife becoming the persuader of her husband to disregard God's voice.

Whenever we dare bypass God given leadership, whether it is in our homes or our local churches, you can know that the spirit of error is at work. Stop it at all cost – it will demolish families and local churches.

The Generation Gap Method

Some say there is a generational gap in our society and churches. The devil has promoted this idea for some time to almost perfection.

Have you noticed that a newborn baby and its mother communicate very well? Mothers will tell you they know exactly what the child wants based on the type of cry they have. Even though there is a gap in their ages of around twenty to thirty years, they still understand each other. To watch the closeness of a mother and her child is amazing.

When a child gets into the public educational system the doctrine of the Generation Gap begins. Many teachers and school leaders in the system begin to tell their students that their parents do not understand them. They say these older people lived during a different time, so they cannot relate to how they feel because they do not have up-to-date understanding for life. By the time children grow into their teen years they are pumped full of this thought and most begin to believe it.

Satan is trying to remove godly parents as the leaders of their children. If teachers and school administrators believed parents were best for the job, they would send the children home for guidance and not refer them to school counselors or other professional psychologists. Many deceived parents believe it is the responsibility of the government to handle the principle setting of the child. They think they are not qualified because they are not educated enough to understand child development – or so they are told.

In addition, the entertainment industry is wedging the generation gap wider in television programs, movies, books, magazines, the music industry, and in radio programming. To these groups parental authority is all but dead. Rebellion against authority flourishes in these environments.

Students look at teachers, school officials, parents, pastors, and other authority as the enemy. If this thinking finds life in the church, we are in for a rocky road. Many are already facing this challenge. However, God wants all ages to work as one unit.

There is a reason we are not all the same age. God has designed age differences in the church as part of His spiritual economy. If we tamper with it and separate the age groups, we will be promoting a breeding ground for false doctrine. Separation of age groups removes necessary elements for the health of the church.

Each generation has something to contribute to the whole. Children and youth are in the church so we will have a sense of discovery fueled by energy. Middle-aged folks show us how to work together. The older generation is there for guidance to those in discovery and to give wisdom for building relationships in the younger generations.

Separated, the older generation gets bitter because the younger are not hearing any instruction. At the same time, the younger get frustrated because the "old folks" are always trying to channel their discovery and scrutinize their friendships.

Through the Generation Gap Method of deception, the older generation stops their necessary influence in the church. They could be a great asset to younger men and women, instead, they have fallen for the lie that their understanding is outdated and their ways are gone with their youth.

Those in the middle age group who are starting and maintaining families are at a loss at how to establish unity because many never observed it growing up.

Many churches have separated the youth from the rest of the congregation. It all starts when they are small children. Taken away from the adult population they are entertained and told a few Bible stories. They certainly learn how to have fun and they find Bible stories have nothing to do with how their families live, giving the Bible a fairy tale impression. God becomes distant with no personal impact. They act out Bible stories instead of learning to follow the Holy Ghost and write their own God-breathed histories.

It is dangerous to keep children and youth away from the adult population. In this system, they rarely tag along with an elder modeling the reality of the power of God, whether it is their parents or someone else in the church. They hear stories either of the past or what will come in the future – never living by faith right now. This may not be the case for every church body, but many are facing this error right now.

Children will never learn about Jesus until we show them what it means to live and walk in the Spirit. This produces events and blessings that prove Jesus is real. They will then follow our example of living by faith in God faster then if we just tell them what to do.

As children reach their teen years, this routine continues. They have their own services, prayer meetings, and planning sessions. However, children and youth need to be in on the work of God with their parents and other members of the Body of Christ. At first it is just observation by being there. Then, gradually they will become part of the work. If they do not, what happens next can be disastrous.

When they graduate from high school, get a job, get married, and thrust into the adult population, they have no idea how to act because they did not mature with the older saints in the church, consequently, they do not know or understand them. This is the result of the Generation Gap Method of deception taught by the world's system of belief.

Now the impact of separation begins to show. They do not know how to spread the gospel to their neighbors. It is not a priority because they get whatever they want through entertainment. Much of what they learned is how to have fun with the crowd, not how to reach for lost souls.

They really want to fit in with the world's ways of living, not "forced" to live a life separated for the work of the Lord. In addition, they have no idea how to disciple someone in the church because they have not been trained by example. Each group is to themselves trying to survive and grow as a group, not as the entire body of Christ.

We have looked everywhere to find a specialist to teach our children and youth and have overlooked the one God put there in the beginning – God-fearing parents.

Part 2
Confronting Error

Chapter 5
Spiritual Adultery

Satan has a plan to destroy the entire church by attacking every person in the body of Christ with his deception. He loves to see a leader fall, but he also works to stop anyone who has been born into the kingdom of God, even those newly born again.

Satan knows the potential of the Word of truth practiced by a believer. He also knows the sin potential in our flesh when awakened. This is why the Apostle John gives us the following warning:

> "Love not the world, neither the things that are in the world. If any man love the world, the love of the Father is not in him. For all that is in the world, the lust of the flesh, and the lust of the eyes, and the pride of life, is not of the Father, but is of the world. And the world passeth away, and the lust thereof: but he that doeth the will of God abideth for ever" (1 John 2:15-17).

If members of the body of Christ ever begin to love anything other than Jesus Christ, they have entered into spiritual adultery.

If we position people, places, or things before God, we will worship them. What we love we worship, what we worship we praise, and what we praise becomes evident to all.

In these verses, John gives us insight into how the world system operates. He gives us *three rules of all carnal behaviors* revealed in sinful lifestyles.

These three rules of carnality are, (1) the lusts of the flesh, (2) the lust of the eyes, and (3) the pride of life. These are man's natural desires operating outside of their God-given and intended use.

Let's look at our God-given desires that the devil has perverted (changed). First, our bodies get hungry and thirsty and we will go to great lengths to satisfy this fleshly desire. Sexual desire is also God given. This is nothing to be embarrassed about, because it has come from God as natural, so we would multiply on the face of the earth.

Secondly, God wanted us to appreciate His creation. He gave us eyes to notice the splendor of a snow-capped mountain range or the beauty of an opened rose.

Thirdly, all human beings have an intense will to save human life. We all have a natural reaction to dangerous situations. When we see something flying at our head we automatically move out of the way. God has placed this reflex in us to save our lives. We also put our own lives in danger to save another life. Each family does not have to look very far to find a story of someone risking their own life to save someone else. God put this automatic preservation of life in every person.

Therefore, we see God has created us with desires of the flesh and eyes and the need to preserve life. This is where Satan, the god of this world, enters to distort and pervert these natural desires and turns them to lusts and pride. This was his motive with Eve in the Garden of Eden.

Look closely at the following verse revealing Satan's use of the three principles of carnality.

"And when the woman saw that the tree *was* good for food, and that it *was* pleasant to the eyes, and a tree to be desired to make *one* wise, she took of the fruit thereof, and did eat, and gave also unto her husband with her; and he did eat" ([Genesis 3:6] underscoring by author).

The Serpent used Eve's natural desire for food, the ability to see pleasant fruit, and the promotion of self-exaltation to deceive her.

Human desire is like a river. Without its banks, you will not discern a river at all. This occurs when the river gets an over-abundance of water, from rains or melting snow, and then over-flows its banks. It is the same with our natural desires. Satan de-sires to take our God-given desires and add an overabundance of stimulation until it overflows its banks.

As an example, visual stimulation of violence and pornogra-phy causes us to act out what we see. We will begin to do what we have seen by over-stimulating our desire until they become sinful actions.

Satan distorts our desire to save human life by refocusing our attention only on our own life and our own preservation. He soon has us convinced that everyone else is our enemy and we must use all of our energy to protect our interests. This begins the ascent into pride and selfishness. He teaches us that our life is our own and no one has any say-so in what we are or what we do.

Fruitfulness or Barrenness?

All plants in their original state reproduce a duplicate of themselves. If you plant corn, you get corn. Sound doctrine pro-duces the fruit of the Spirit and false doctrine produces the works of the flesh. It is that simple.

When a church body is in the will of God, it will produce the fruit of the Spirit, which makes a thriving church. On the other hand, spiritual barrenness comes from man's wisdom. It may not appear spiritually barren if you judge from a carnal viewpoint. Many are "thriving" in man-made success and never realize they are spiritually barren. Only God can reveal barrenness; only truth reveals error.

Spiritual barrenness is people remaining the same – they never mature. It is when the power of God becomes ineffective in changing people from sinners to saints. Barrenness is people not receiving the Holy Ghost in our churches. Barrenness is seeing the majority of our youth walk away from God as they grow into adulthood. It is hiding fornication, adultery, alcoholism, and drug addiction (including prescription drugs), pornography, lying, cheating, stealing and yet professing love for Jesus Christ.

We can busy ourselves with how we raise money, program a church service, or get a visitor to come to our church building, but never find the way to change the heart of man. This is barrenness – busy barrenness.

Man can do many great things and appear like everything is under control. Man's ways can fool you – he is a great achiever. It is possible to see greatness "done in the name of Jesus" but actually being accomplished by the will of man. Just look under the surface of this so-called success and you will find a mess.

Stories of man's achievements surround us. Many have built great church buildings, cathedrals, and temples, but this does not mean they are in the will of God. It does not mean it is for His purpose or following His pattern for the Church, which is sanctification (set apart only for God's use).

The fire of judgment will destroy everything built of an earthly nature. Only those who have built on the true foundation of the Apostles, Prophets, and the Cornerstone of Jesus Christ, will stand (Ephesians 2:19-22).

Man's wisdom brings divisions and strife to the church. If man does it, he demands credit. If more than one individual determines the credit belongs to them, the fight commences.

In the book of James, chapter four he asks, "From whence come wars and fightings among you? Come they not hence, even of your lusts that war in your members?"

People who live by the lust of their flesh will always live miserable lives. The flesh is never satisfied; it always wants more. Unsatisfied people are always fighting with one another, no one gets what they want, and no one gets their way. It's like having a room full of two and three year olds in adult bodies. They are not mature enough to understand their place in the body of Christ. They have forgotten what defines greatness in the Kingdom of God.

It is not about being better than others to get the applause of the group. It is about becoming like the Master, Jesus Christ. He showed His disciples the power of being a servant when He washed their feet during the Passover supper before His trial and death. The Greatest became the servant to us all.

An immature group of people will be self-willed, full of envy and debate always clawing for more territory to rule over. When things are not going their way, you will hear from them – mark it down.

James went on to say, "Ye lust, and have not: ye kill, and desire to have, and cannot obtain: ye fight and war, yet ye have not, because ye ask not. Ye ask, and receive not, because ye ask amiss, that ye may consume it upon your lusts."

At this point, we should remember James is speaking to the church, not those outside of the body of Christ. We must hear this warning and do a personal inventory of the motivation in our lives. Are we motivated by the lust of the flesh and eyes, along with the pride of life, or by faith, hope, and love? If it is the first group, we are on the path of error. Before long, we will be where we never intended to go.

Do not be surprised at the depths of evil Satan convinces people to go on their way down into apostasy. Tongues become loaded with bitterness and weary minds filled with distrust. It all leads to evil works. It may not be on the surface, but under it, you will find abuse, accusation, temper tantrums, disrespect, and distrust, along with a number of other controlling behaviors. It is because they cannot have what they want.

James then turned his attention to spiritual adultery in verse four, "Ye adulterers and adulteresses, know ye not that the friendship of the world is enmity with God? Whosoever therefore will be a friend of the world is the enemy of God. Do ye think that the scripture saith in vain, The spirit that dwelleth in us lusteth to envy?"

Flirting with the gods of the world system causes this condition of spiritual adultery and is dangerous. Eventually you will become what you love. Individuals in the body of Christ cannot act like a flirting harlot. Israel played this game and got herself in bondage, even to this day.

We cannot play both lovers – God is jealous of his church. When we begin to play with another lover, the Holy Ghost will make us miserable. The grouchiest people you will find are those who try to serve God and mammon (earthly valuables). God will make them uncomfortable until they repent – turning themselves fully back to Him.

"God resisteth the proud, but giveth grace unto the humble. Submit yourselves therefore to God. Resist the devil, and he will flee from you. Draw nigh to God, and he will draw nigh to you. Cleanse your hands, ye sinners; and purify your hearts, ye double minded," James went on to say.

Double mindedness will never overcome the adversary. Humility and submission to the hand of the Lord will bring the mercy of God to us. In the position of submission to God our resistance against the devil will work – he will flee from us.

Chapter 6
Apostasy and Its First Step: Replacing Godly Standards

"Now the Spirit speaketh expressly, that in the latter times some shall depart from the faith, giving heed to seducing spirits, and doctrines of devils; Speaking lies in hypocrisy; having their conscience seared with a hot iron;" (1 Timothy 4:1,2)

The word apostasy is only in the original Greek New Testament, but the apostolic writers mention this theme often in our English translations. It means a falling away, a withdrawal, or to defect from the faith. It is unbelief.

Once you have turned from sin (repented), been baptized in Jesus' name and received the Holy Ghost, speaking in tongues, you are in danger of apostasy. Satan wants to destroy your obedience to the Word of God illuminated by the Spirit.

This author has observed three basic steps of apostasy. They are, (1) the replacement of godly standards, (2) learning to cope with a sinful lifestyle, and (3) loosing the revelation of Jesus Christ. They are progressive steps down and linked together. Those who go into apostasy pass through each one until they reach the third step, which is the loss of the revelation of Jesus

Christ. This final step is denying Jesus for who He really is.

The First Step of Apostasy: The Replacement of Godly Standards

The word "standard" has become an evil word to many religious systems today. Talking about standards has become a forbidden issue for many, but the church needs to reopen the discussion.

To spiritually destroy individuals and families in a local assembly the devil does not shove us over a cliff into false beliefs and a sinful lifestyle. He uses small steps down instead. His first step is to remove your godly standards, replace them with his standards, and make sure you never realize the switch. In addition, he definitely does not want you to use the "forbidden" word – standards.

We should not be afraid of the word standard. All standards are set for us to compare ourselves to them. You either match the standard or disregard it. Standards are rules, principles or values. Standards are everywhere, and they will always be important to establish guidelines for living. The key is to select the right set of standards.

Certain jobs have a standard of dress or a dress code. Public education has academic standards. There are also standards of protocol (codes of behavior) in the United States government. Standards are set in every institution and organization by the leadership to project a certain image or achieve a desired result. If the members do not match these standards, disciplinary action usually follows. On the other hand, if enough people rebel against the rules, gradually new standards are established or old ones are relaxed or transformed.

If individuals in the church become uneasy when the word standard is used you can know Satan has done a good job implementing this first step of apostasy in their lives. If he is successful in making us "drop the subject," he then can push his standards of living. He will blast home the command, "conform to your environment!" He doesn't call them standards, he calls it, "being accepted in the group."

We might as well relax; the church will always have standards. God has not left us without something to guide the way we live.

* * * *

Years ago, the United States, along with several other countries, had the gold standard. This standard kept the price fixed on the value of gold. There was enough gold to back all printed currency. During the economic crisis of 1929 and the ensuing depression, most countries along with the U.S. found it necessary to abandon the standard so they could produce more currency due to high inflation. The U.S. used a modified standard of $35 per ounce of gold. They needed more currency than they had gold to back it. In essence, they began borrowing against the future earnings of the American people. By 1975, the U.S. began to sell its gold on the open market. Gold moved from being a standard (having a fixed price) to becoming a commodity. Now, the price of gold can fluctuate up or down depending on the supply and demand in the open market. It no longer has a fixed value.

Have God's standards become a commodity to be "bought and sold?" Have they lost their value as an absolute standard to live by? Has the new economy of religion forced us to devalue God's principles and only use it when we want or need it? Has religious "inflation" caused us to look for more than one way to conduct our Christian lives?

Do we use our "church" standards only when we are with those who believe a certain way and then change to a different value with someone else? Do the standards change based on new ideas from a more "advanced" church?

Satan loves change as long as it is away from the principles established by God to any other standard for living.

The devil keeps the world churning out new standards all the time so people will be accustomed to no set standard. He teaches people to identify with any standard they want – whatever feels or looks good to them at the time. Remember, everyone lives by some standard.

Satan has also convinced some in the church to churn out so many different standards until we become convinced there should be no set standard for God's people. We can become convinced that standards are personal convictions and not common to all. Surely, Jesus Christ came to deliver us from personal preferences, not splinter us into conservative and liberal groups with their own set of standards.

If God's Word, spoken or read, convicts you about something you are doing, you must stop. If you happen to see it practiced by another brother or sisters, the devil will attempt to convince you it is not a sin to them. He continues his lie by saying, "It is just your personal conviction, not for anyone else, so don't push it on anyone else."

It is as if everyone has their own ability to discern right from wrong on their own without listening to the Holy Ghost, studying the Word of God, or pastoral authority. Personal convictions then dictate the standards for their lifestyles, leaving no other authority but themselves.

Personal convictions are just that, personal to the individual – what is right for them alone. Anyone can claim a personal conviction and dare authority to touch it. Beware; this is rebellion.

We cannot use Paul's statement that he was "all things to all men" (1 Corinthians 9:22) as an argument to change our standards of living to be acceptable to those around us. Paul did not believe in blending paganism with the church. He did, however, know the secret of reaching people with the gospel – be a servant to all men that you might win some. There is a vast difference between a servant and a chameleon.

This idea of individually selected standards leaves many faced with no warning if a spirit of error sneaks into their lives. Teachers that propagate the gospel of personal convictions can say nothing when error comes. After all, personal convictions are supposed to take care of it. This lazy approach to spiritual leadership will have a time of reaping that is very painful.

This approach never gives warnings like, "please be careful, you are listening to the wrong voices" or, "you are being lead away from God's purpose by your lifestyle."

"These are negative and harmful words," or they say, "It will drive people away." Therefore, you will never share what God has revealed to you about sin because Satan has deceived you that it is not for anyone else. By the way, how would the Epistles read if the writers did not corrected any errors they saw in the churches? Furthermore, doesn't biblical correction apply to us also?

Churches are taking this step of replacing godly standards every day. This step is actually away from God's purpose, although it may not appear like it on the surface. The disaster of apostasy lies ahead.

This is Satan's first step. It attacks the outward appearance and lifestyle differences in the saints. Satan has fought apostolic people relentlessly for years on this subject. The phrase, "God doesn't care how I look or what I do," is a lie. He does care. It really does make a difference.

Has someone tried to convince you that the church is foolish for having a different standard of appearance and lifestyle? Have voices told you that your principles are from the past and not for the modern generation?

The devil has hammered on it until many people do not know what to believe any more. Many feel too intimidated to touch the "hot potato" of appearance and lifestyle standards. They say it is too messy and confusing.

This sustained debate and confusion reveals that Satan is in the picture. He does not want local churches or family units to use any standards or principles God has instituted. He does not want people believing that God has a design for us to live by.

Remember, standards can be right and wrong. God has standards and so does the world system, controlled by Satan — the father of lies.

Satan has lied to many people by telling them to go out of the church where there are no standards. However, there are standards outside of the church as well as inside the church. There are rules of conduct in this world to be a part of the system. Unless you look and act a certain way, you are an outsider and not accepted. Everyone will comply with some standard for living.

Gangs, prostitutes, bikers, and rock star fans (groupies) have standards. Models, movie and television stars, stage performers, fashion designers, and sports heroes along with many other groups, set the standards that the world lives by. People do what their heroes do.

Then there are false teachers trying to convince us we should not have any standards at all in the church. This is a standard in its own right. You still are going to dress a certain way, go places for activities, be with certain kinds of people, and accumulate certain things, no matter what they say.

Standards, good or bad, are guidelines to produce a desired outcome. There are even standards being set to make the church blend with its local environment by many religious groups. This is a standard adopted throughout the centuries to make "Christianity" acceptable to the heathen masses.

There are standards to fulfill the lust of the flesh and eyes and the pride of life. These are Satan's rules that lead to sin and death.

Then there are standards that fulfill the law of Christ. The Law of Christ is love. We do not wear some things because of love. We do not give all of our time to pleasures because it leads to idolatry. There are places we do not go because of love, people we do not become intimate with because of love, and things we do not acquire because of love. We must not break the principle of love. Jesus commanded us to love our neighbor as we love ourselves. If anything promotes a breaking of the Law of God, we must get rid of it.

> Owe no man any thing, but to love one another: for he that loveth another hath fulfilled the law. For this, Thou shalt not commit adultery, Thou shalt not kill, Thou shalt not steal, Thou shalt not bear false witness, Thou shalt not covet; and if *there be* any other commandment, it is briefly comprehended in this saying, namely, Thou shalt love thy neighbour as thyself. Love worketh no ill to his neighbour: therefore love *is* the fulfilling of the law" (Romans 13:8-10).

Why would a person want to paint up, dress up, and behave in such a manner to get the attention of the opposite sex? They wouldn't unless they desired the attention. Wanting to capture the attention of someone else by how we appear reveals the intent of the heart. It also reveals a standard used to achieve the goal.

Our love for God dictates our standards. Our love for the body of Christ causes us to live by godly principles. Our love for the lost drives us to live by a different standard so they can come to a different way of life. The true church is different from the world – we will never fit in.

When people become confused about what defines sin, this reveals the loss of the standard of measurement. Jesus said concerning the Law of God, "Thou shalt love the Lord thy God with all thy heart, and with all thy soul, and with all thy mind. This is the first and great commandment. And the second *is* like unto it, Thou shalt love thy neighbour as thyself. On these two commandments hang all the law and the prophets" (Matthew 22:37-40). Jesus revealed that all you have to do is match what you were doing against the standard of these two commandments and you will see whether you are living right.

The Law of God given to Moses is the standard of measurement that proves all men are sinners. This standard makes the need for a Savior very real. Until then, you can pick any standard to live by. However, after the awareness of our sinful condition, picking any standard will not do. We must have Jesus Christ's new standard in our lives to be righteous.

The only way to establish His standard in our lives is to receive the gift of the Holy Ghost, be baptized in Jesus' name and then follow the leading of the Spirit and the Word in His Body of believers.

If we live and walk in the Spirit, we will not live a sinful lifestyle (see Chapter 12 for an in-depth look at following the leading of the Holy Ghost).

Chapter 7
Step Two: Coping With Sinful Lifestyles

Learning to cope with a sinful lifestyle is the second step down in the process of apostasy. The first step down discussed in the previous chapter was the deceptive replacement of godly standards with any standard available in the world. Satan does not care which standard of living you choose as long as it is not Jesus' standard of stopping sin before it makes itself at home in your mind, producing sinful actions. Anything that causes you to sin is also a sin to have and to hold.

Living in a room full of poisonous snakes is dangerous. One bite may not kill you, but with a room full of snakes around you, the chances of repeated hits and eventual death is very real.

Learning to live with these snakes is not the way to keep away from their fangs. Getting rid of them is what reduces the risk to almost nothing. The only bite now comes from a hidden snake and most survive a single bite.

We must get rid of all things that lead to sin. Clean house by the power of the Holy Ghost you have received and see the difference. Again, if it causes us to sin, it is a sin to have around.

Satan always attempts to teach Holy Ghost filled people to ignore and override the leading of the Spirit. God will prick our hearts with a feeling of conviction when we are about to sin, not just after we sin. This is the finger of God touching the very center of us, letting us know we have wrong intentions. When we override our obedience to the leading of the Spirit we are sinning. Unrepentant sin plunges us into guilt, which makes us miserable people.

Satan is coaching us to overpower conviction. He does this by using the philosophy, "Don't let anyone make you feel guilty."

The Liar wants us to blame sinning on external circumstances beyond our control. Instead of taking responsibility of turning from sin, the enemy wants us to cover up the feelings of guilt and never place our sin under the blood of Jesus Christ. He does not want us to stop doing what produces the guilt, just learn to cope with it.

It seems each week he invents new excuses for us to justify our repeated sinning against God and new psychology to manage the guilt. The natural next step in apostasy is the loss of true repentance.

Some people give the impression that living a life of repetitive sinning is natural – even in the church. Church congregations living this way are going to be a guilt ridden church and in need of constant counseling. These people never feel deliverance from the guilt of sin. They simply have lost the true meaning of repentance – they repeat their sins and find ways to comfort themselves in their guilt.

For many the word repentance does not mean what John the Baptist, Jesus Christ, and the Apostles taught it to mean.

Satan's replacement for true repentance is *penance*. Penance is not repentance. The definition of penance is confession of sin and forgiveness of it. Over the centuries, the word repentance has acquired this new meaning of penance for many. Masses of people have gone "forward" in a church and prayed for forgiveness of their sins only to leave the building and repeat the sins. They then return the next week to submerge the guilt of repetitive sinning in the same "feel good" religious ritual. No one told them to *stop* the repetitive sinning. All they know is to keep asking God to forgive them for their cycle of sinning. In reality, there is no value in asking God to forgive you if you continue to do the sin.

Many people are returning to their church week after week to go through the same ceremony of asking God to forgive them for the same sins. This is a way to find comfort or to relieve the stress of guilt caused by sin. However, this is not repentance.

Satan has labored to remove the true meaning of repentance from the church and give a counterfeit, all the while leaving the word repentance in our vocabulary, but not the proper actions to go along with it.

Repentance means, a change of mind, of purpose, and direction. Repentance occurs when someone has had enough sorrow of living in sin and turns around to walk with Jesus Christ as the leader of their lives.

Simply put, if a person truly repents, they stop the lifestyle of sinning. Sin is no longer the master of their life – they are free of the bondage of sin. Jesus has become the Master that gives 100% direction. They live by a different set of standards.

As discussed earlier, Satan's plan is to convince us that we can live by any standard we choose. If any standard is acceptable then there is no need to preach repentance anymore. There is no definite standard. All you have to do is learn to deal with the guilt caused by sinning. This is how penance comes in handy. You can do it as often as you need to without stopping the sin.

No matter what anyone tells you, all sinners will live with guilt. God has designed us to feel guilt when we sin. Satan then uses guilt as a weapon against the churches that are preaching the truth. When people feel guilt, they frown and feel downcast, and who wants to be in a church of miserable people? Satan then pushes the message of low self-esteem. He tells us to just make the people feel better. But, it is a trap being set that we must never walk into.

We will have to find a carnal means to give the sinner a "lift" if we do not tell them the truth about repentance. Stopping the things that bring guilt is the greatest relief any person can feel. Repentance (an about-face from sinning), baptism in Jesus' name, and receiving the gift of the Holy Ghost, speaking in tongues, and then becoming obedient to the leading of the Spirit is God's will for humanity. This new birth process removes the condemnation of sin and frees us from its penalty.

To understand repentance we must move from the idea of merely being sorry for our sin to abandoning sin. Grief of sin does not necessarily make us stop. A person can be sorry they sinned without the decision to abandon the practices. Stopping sins in our lives is repentance. This is victorious living — freedom from the bondage of sin. Furthermore, it is possible to break free from a lifestyle of sinning.

Many argue that no one is perfect and grace allows us to live a sinful life. God forbid.

> What shall we say then? Shall we continue in sin, that grace may abound? God forbid. How shall we, that are dead to sin, live any longer therein" (Romans 6:1,2)?

After Satan gets your appearance and lifestyle to blend with one of the many worldly standards, he now has a hold on your moral condition. You will begin to tolerate promiscuity, homosexual lifestyles, ungodly jokes, abortions, addictions, and many other bondages and ways of Satan's system. This is because he controls your mind. Whoever influences the mind is the ruler of the lifestyle. He will lead you by fleshly desires and teach you to live with the guilt of sin by involving you in even more pleasures in the "world" of bondages. If he can get you to cope with a room full of poisonous snakes, he has you in the trap.

Now you are identifying with and practicing the principles of sinful humanity. He knows he has you thinking with a carnal mind and you will begin to do the things of a carnal person. You now will begin to fulfill the lust of the flesh and eyes and live by the pride of life.

> "Now the works of the flesh are manifest, which are *these*; Adultery, fornication, uncleanness, lasciviousness, Idolatry, witchcraft, hatred, variance, emulations, wrath, strife, seditions, heresies, Envyings, murders, drunkenness, revellings, and such like: of the which I tell you before, as I have also told *you* in time past, that they which do such things shall not inherit the kingdom of God" (Galatians 5:19-21).

Now you will begin to move toward the worship of other gods more easily because you have selected wrong standards and learned to bury your guilt in pleasures.

Then, Satan teaches you to reject anyone who lives by godly principles. He will teach you to be a scoffer, making fun of the "poor souls" who are lonely legalist forcing people to serve God "their way."

If you have the baptism of the Holy Ghost and you are about to sin there is a prick in your heart. An uncomfortable feeling comes over you and you begin to feel miserable until you overcome the temptation. If you do not arrest the thought and it becomes sin, you really have a stirring of the Spirit inside now. The Holy Ghost and sin do not mix. God is a jealous God. He will not give you up without a fight.

Satan now moves in rapidly to advise you that anyone who makes you feel bad or guilty is out of line with the grace and mercy of God. "No one is perfect, so leave them alone," you will hear.

The field of Psychology often deals with the issue of how we feel about ourselves. The leaders in this field propose that if anyone makes you feel bad or guilty, they are wrong. They teach you to stay away from these negative people, and find groups that make you feel accepted and comfortable.

The rational goes something like this, "Everyone is a sinner so no one is qualified to preach against sin." This is when you will hear the "no one is perfect" story and, "Jesus loves you just the way you are." Jesus does love you the way you are, but that is not the issue. If we do not stop our repetitive sinning, we will face the judgment of God – that is the issue.

Repeating the words, "I accept Jesus' grace, mercy, and love," has replaced true repentance. This is a great way to get people off your back. Many Sunday night altars, even in Apostolic churches, have replaced repentance with penance. It appears to get God and the preacher off your back; after all, they see the emotions.

After the devil gets us into a cycle of penance, never allowing us to stop the repetitive sinning he has won a victory. Then we move into the second part of this step down.

Preachers stop preaching repentance and start saying, "You

need to get help for your problem." They will not tell you to stop sinning because they have no idea of how to make you stop. They are deceived into thinking there may be a good reason why you cannot stop sinning.

The cycle of counseling now begins. The devil begins his attack on the preacher by telling him he is not qualified to help these miserable souls out of their problems. The preacher then goes to school to learn how to be a good counselor.

Where do you think the devil directs him to go? Naturally, to someone who does not believe in biblical principles. Sometimes you will find someone who claims to be a Christian counselor. However, true Christian counselors do not use a forked tongue approach. They will not give you humanistic views and godly views mixed together. God's way is to only use His Word and the gifts of the Spirit to truly help the person find deliverance. If we do not know the difference between godly and earthly wisdom, look out, the spirit of error is present.

Most repeat counseling sessions would be nonexistent if we understood and used the God-given concept of repentance. People are looking for this deliverance.

First, we must be 100% responsible for 100% of our actions, and then teach others the same. Otherwise, we are allowing a loophole.

Committing a sin and living a sinful lifestyle are two different things. All people were born in sin and everyone has sinned, but not everyone lives a sinful lifestyle. There are people who have been set free from the bondage of sin. Bondage is doing the same sin repeatedly. Freedom is breaking free of the sinning cycle.

The church is currently being pressured into not preaching about a complete change of life. People want to learn how to cope with sin, but we must never learn to comfortably coexist with sinful lifestyles.

This is an area where modern psychology has made a huge impact. Psychology is the study of human behavior. It is humans looking at humans. Man does not have the capacity to fully understand himself. This is why Satan has used the field of psychology to ruin many good people. If you enter this field of learning you will be schooled by people who use man's wisdom to instruct you. Remember, man can't figure out what is wrong with himself. The created (man) must appeal solely to the Creator (God) for guidance.

Psychology textbooks and periodicals have replaced God's Word and the gifts of the Spirit for some, and the trend is growing. More time is spent reading and studying about the problems of man instead of prayerful surrender of our own lives to God. Through our personal brokenness of falling on the Rock, we become a conduit of God's wisdom and power. His Word reveals the thoughts and intents of the heart and His Spirit brings discernment of the man's spirit.

If we learn to cope with sin, this is when the baptism of the Holy Ghost, as received on the Day of Pentecost, becomes obsolete. It now can be easily relegated as a past phenonmenon, only for the early church, and placed in a museum.

We then are actually learning to live without the guidance of the Holy Ghost. If this guidance is no longer needed our doctrine will change to reflect the "uselessness" of the Holy Ghost.

Now, easy believism will replace the truth of the gospel message. Everyone will only have to say they are sorry for being a sinner and nothing more. No one will be able to tell how sorry, because a lifestyle change is no longer demanded.

It's sad, but many people just show up at the church building, give a little money, try not to cause too much trouble, be on a committee or two, and then live the way they want to live. They don't have to worry about living by godly standards – picking any standard they want has become the way of life for them, and many churches just leave them alone.

Chapter 8
Step Three: Loss of the Revelation of Jesus Christ

The question, "Who is Jesus?" embodies the third step down into apostasy. This question may seem unthinkable for those who treasure their revelation of Jesus Christ, but it is a deception of Satan to take away the power of Jesus' name by clouding His identity.

As Christianity first began, it faced pressure to blend with the pagan practices surrounding them. The Gentile nations were believers in many gods (polytheism). This caused the church, which was transitioning from a Jewish to a Gentile church, to feel pressure to permit more than one God into their belief system. They wanted to embrace both their old lifestyles and gods along with this new exciting Christianity.

From the death of the Apostles to around 300-400 A.D., the church went into a slide of apostasy. We know this because they began to argue about who Jesus really was – His identity had become foggy. They even had the Council of Nicea in 325 A.D. to determine who He was and later "clarified" their thoughts with later councils. They were confused because they had taken the other steps away from the revelation of Jesus Christ, as discussed in the last two chapters. The problem rested on their blending of

Christianity into an appealing religious system for Gentiles by allowing sinful practices instead of true repentance from their pagan gods, evil rituals, and sinful lifestyles.

The revelation of Jesus Christ is more than a simple belief that He existed as a figure in history who's story needs passed down from generation to generation. Jesus came to do more than become famous – He came to save us from sin. This is why Satan has attacked the true message of liberation from sin and promoted serving other gods and pagan practices.

As the Jewish apostolic church faded and transitioned into a Gentile church, the absence of the Jewish voice, which demanded that God is one, gave way to the heathen practices of polytheism (belief in multiple gods). However, God did not leave it this way.

God has always had a body of true believers, but in the early 1900's, the revelation of the Almighty God in Jesus Christ began to emerge throughout the world on a grand scale. People began to see that God is not a trinity of persons. They saw that Jesus was the only person that expressed and revealed the great I AM. Jesus said when you saw Him you actually were seeing the Father. This is because Jesus was the only begotten Son of God. He was the only flesh of God – the only person of God. This revelation came because people were receiving the gift of the Holy Ghost, speaking in tongues, and abandoning their sinful practices through the leading of the Spirit, they had just received.

This is why it is one of the saddest days in church history when someone who once believed God to be one Spirit manifested in one body of Jesus Christ, is deceived to believe there are three persons of God. The error of "God the Father, God the Son, and God the Holy Ghost" has swept the religious world.

Those who leave the truth of the oneness of God and move to the man-made model of three persons of God have only done so by the cunning of Satan which gradually erodes the truth.

God is self-existent. By Himself He is the Creator of all things and powers. God is the only Savior. God declares in His Word there is no other God formed before Him or after Him. There simply is no "room" for another God because He fills everything. Jesus Christ was not a part of God, but was God revealing (manifesting) Himself in the body of a man. The flesh is the

Son of God not God the Son. Furthermore, Jesus Christ had a beginning. He was not eternally the Son of God. He was born in Bethlehem. He was the only begotten Son (flesh) of God. Begotten is born of and denotes a beginning – Jesus was born of a women by the Word of God. In the flesh (Son), dwelt all the fullness of God. Jesus was the manifestation of the invisible God.

This false belief of Jesus Christ being a third person of God can only come about because He is no longer needed for who He really is. Jesus was born into the world to break the bondage of sin and claim the keys of death and its holding place called Hell. The name given to Jesus reveals His purpose.

> "And she shall bring forth a son, and thou shalt call his name JESUS: for he shall save his people from their sins" (Matthew 1:21).

* * * *

Once again, let's look at the progression down through the steps of apostasy. (1) If any standard of living is okay to adopt as our own and, (2) if we then learn to cope with our sinful condition, we will then enter the next stage of apostasy – (3) loosing our revelation of who Jesus is.

We loose our revelation because we no longer need Jesus to be a Savior – we are convinced any lifestyle is acceptable and we no longer need saved from anything. The purpose of Jesus Christ is to seek and save the lost. However, if we are okay the way we are, we have devalued the price of the blood and the power of the name of Jesus. We no longer need the power of the blood of Jesus.

Many people are professing the name of Jesus yet trampling its true meaning under foot. They are defiling the Precious Name by making it powerless through their rebellion. Their use of Jesus' name is in vain because they have refused the revealed meaning – Jesus saves people *from* their sins.

God will bring judgment upon all who do not have a love for the truth with swift destruction. We desecrate the name of Jesus when we use it for any other purpose than the salvation of man's soul from a sinful life. Do not devalue the Name by saying a prayer of penance and returning to the mire of sin only to go back to more ceremonial hype attempting to cover guilt with a religious pat on the back.

Once you forget Jesus' purpose for coming to this earth, you will no longer understand who He is. You are now ready to believe in the man-made concept of God as a trinity or some other form of false doctrine. God will become distant and unknowable and you will fall for the deception of placing God in an unreachable mystery. The revelation of the Mighty God in Jesus Christ will die and finite science will attempt to define the living God. However, this is impossible because the carnal mind or the wisdom of the world will never define God.

This process strips revelation from the common person and places the "understanding" of God in the hands of a few privileged by seminary study. An intellectual elite guard cannot hold the revelation of Jesus Christ hostage by spiritual blindness. This gospel is universal. All people, regardless of social, economical, educational, or racial standing, can know Jesus Christ as Lord of their lives.

Jesus Christ is the only One who defines God. To know Jesus is to know God. If we loose this understanding, we will die in our sins (John 8:24).

* * * *

To receive truth it must be uncovered. Truth is not innate nor is it automatic. The cover has to be pulled back to reveal what has been there all the time.

> "And without controversy great is the mystery of godliness: God was manifest in the flesh, justified in the Spirit, seen of angels, preached unto the Gentiles, believed on in the world, received up into glory" (1 Timothy 3:16).

It is amazing how people get a "un-revelation." If God has showed you something about Himself He does not take it away from you. Do not allow the cunning craftiness of man's wisdom fueled by the deception of the devil, to derail your simple faith that was first delivered to you.

We are to grow in faith, not adopt a new faith. Many are looking for a new foundation and cornerstone, but the original is still intact. How are we building on it?

Remember when Peter blurted out, "Thou art the Christ, the son of the living God?" Jesus' reply was, "Flesh and blood hath not revealed it unto thee, but my Father which is in heaven." Jesus was letting Peter know he had a revelation of a covered piece of truth.

When the church looses its hunger for spiritual things, it looses the truth. Hunger for spiritual things die out when we live by fleshly desires. This is the main purpose for Satan's deception in the first two steps of apostasy. He wants us to abandon the spiritual listening ear and turn to a life of fulfilling fleshly desires. We cannot exist only by the flesh and expect to live eternally. Man cannot live by bread alone, but by every Word that proceeds out of the mouth of God. God's Word is Life.

This is the place in apostasy where water baptism in the name of Jesus Christ for the remission of sins becomes meaningless. It now just becomes a non-essential outward sign. In other words, it does not do anything – it is just a ceremony. Water baptism no longer is a necessary part of the revelation of Jesus Christ. The apostate church administers baptism using the titles Father, Son, and Holy Ghost. They do not recognize the saving name of Jesus Christ. This truly is apostasy.

By the time religious organizations have reached this point, a simple phrase captures everything they know concerning Jesus Christ; "I accept the Lord Jesus Christ as my personal savior." They say this embodies the complete plan of God for any individual's salvation. What they fail to see is, that God does not accept their plan no matter how popular it has become. They have abandoned the pattern established by Jesus and the Apostles.

Man-made religion is always meaningless rituals. Men have trampled the truth under foot and designed a god that suits their fleshly desires.

Here is what has happened to the truth for those in apostasy:

- The true meaning of repentance now means penance for the apostate church, so there is no talk of stop-

ping repetitive sin.
- Sin is "gone" because there is no authority to define it.
- Baptism in Jesus' name is not necessary because there is nothing to wash away. Just thank God for his grace and mercy and continue to do what you want to do.
- The Holy Ghost, speaking in tongues, if accepted at all, is still not a necessity for every believer, and looked at as a blessing reserved for a few. In addition, to listen to the leading of the Spirit is not taught or practiced.

Pray that your family and church never end up in this place – this is apostasy.

Part 3
False Prophets

Chapter 9
Beware of False Prophets

"Beware of false prophets, which come to you in sheep's clothing, but inwardly they are ravening wolves" (Matthew 7:15).

We cannot approach the subject of false prophets with, "let someone else worry about it," or "we have the truth so we don't have to worry about false prophets and their doctrine." Through the guidance of the Spirit and the Word, the Body of Christ must work together to detect and reveal false ways.

Jesus told us to beware of false prophets. Included in His warning, were some guidelines to identify them and their false messages.

We cannot have "knee-jerk" responses of agreement with preachers, just because their words sound good. First impressions of a false prophet may be good if we use carnal assessments. Deceivers understand how to use our carnal desires and pride to their benefit. Therefore, we must be careful that our fleshly desires do not block what the Spirit needs to reveal about them.

Agreement Training

One of the first plans a false prophet develops is our agreement with them as quickly as possible — publicly. They will push for quick agreement because they do not want you to ponder their words. To see and hear your agreement is their goal. Visual and verbal responses are important to give the appearance of acceptance to unsuspecting observers. However, do people really agree or have they been trained to appear so?

Their first step is to say things anyone would believe, like, "God is a miracle working God, now don't you agree with that?" The pressure mounts to show outward signs of agreement, like nodding your head in agreement or saying, "amen." Agreement Training works great because it gives the appearance of universal agreement allowing easy insertion of false doctrines.

Here is how it works. False prophets know if you dwell on their words and match them to the Word of God, you will find their error. They desire to control through immediate agreement because hesitation reveals thinkers. Disagreement and questions are a no-no with false prophets. If you do not agree, they often get angry. Their anger then becomes a tool of intimidation. Either you agree or you feel like a fool.

Once this training of agreement to everything they say is in place, they can begin to slip in false phrases while you are agreeing with them, "forcing" you to affirm false doctrine. The aim is your visible or audible agreement to their error, even if you do not agree in your heart. To keep yourself out of "hot water" you just agree out of fear or exhaustion. Eventually, you just nod your head no matter what they are saying to make them happy.

Most people do not recognize this Agreement Training Method of deception. Beware; the devil is cunning in his approach.

The Disguise

Jesus said false prophets are wolves with sheep's clothing on. It is a covering to fool you, making you think the wolf is one of the sheep.

Sheep fear a wolf unless they hide by disguise and blend into the flock. Disguises are always an indication of a false prophet in your presents. They go to great lengths maintaining their cover. They are adept at costuming their real character and real intent. This is why we must understand disguises and Jesus Christ has given us a way.

One way is to observe how they set and teach principles. It is often difficult to know a false prophet's position on any given issue. One disguise they use is "feeling out" your opinions first. After you show your belief, they will agree with you, but beware, it is a lie. They do not want you to see their heart. They want to know what you believe first so they can attempt to draw you away slowly into their way of thinking.

False prophets think they are masters of timing and control, but the Spirit of God is able to give discernment of their tactics. God's people will see through these disguises of evil character and harmful intentions.

You may be fooled for a time, but keep your eyes open, because the wolf has a different appetite than a sheep. He loves to sneak in and catch his prey off guard. Keep a watch; he will eventually reveal what is under the disguise. He always steals, kills, and destroys members of the flock. The wolf loves blood – sheep do not. Also, watch for the source of strife in the church – you will find the carriers of the spirit of error.

False Prophets will preach mercy until they desire you as the victim of their manipulation. You will hear endless messages on love, mercy, and the grace of God until you get in the way of their plan to steal, kill, and destroy. Now you are the enemy and they will pounce on you.

While reading, you may have had the thought cross your mind, *well, I had better be careful not to start a witch-hunt in the church.*

Remember, Satan will try everything he can in his remaining time to discourage you from promoting doctrinal purity in your family and the church. This is not a witch-hunt. We must use Holy Ghost discernment. Do not be afraid of it – use it. Declare war on false doctrine and God will fight for the saints. It is not a fleshly warfare, but a spiritual one that requires spiritual tactics. Do not be intimidated, God will fight for us – He wants truth maintained in the church and declared to the world.

This idea of false doctrine being present in the church can make us feel uncomfortable because it places all of us under scrutiny. This is okay; it is time to take a closer look.

If we do not judge ourselves against the biblical standards God has given us, many people will be lost. It will be ourselves first, then those who hear us.

If you suspect someone is moving toward deception, others will sense it too. Remember, the church is a collaborative effort. You do not have to be a one-person error detection service. God always reveals false prophets to His unified church.

Lovers of truth will always be defenders of it and spot deceptive teaching. When you see error in your local church, begin to bind it in prayer. When it creeps into your family, pray together, study together, and talk together, until the revelation comes from God.

You Will Know Them By Their Fruits

"Ye shall know them by their fruits. Do men gather grapes of thorns, or figs of thistles? Even so every good tree bringeth forth good fruit; but a corrupt tree bringeth forth evil fruit. A good tree cannot bring forth evil fruit, neither *can* a corrupt tree bring forth good fruit. Every tree that bringeth not forth good fruit is hewn down, and cast into the fire. Wherefore by their fruits ye shall know them" (Matthew 7:16-20).

Our Lord gave us another method of detecting false prophets, "Wherefore by their fruits ye shall know them." The simplicity here is easy to overlook.

Over time, you will see the results (fruit) of any leader or local church. Are people in the church repeating the process of overcoming the same sins in their lives for weeks, or months, or years? Alternatively, is there a genuine change in their lives by repentance and the leading of the Holy Ghost? Is there an overall maturing process in the church or are saints becoming confused about basic principles or standards to live by, or about the truth of the oneness of God? Do they detect and stop sins in their lives or have they learned to cope with them?

Confusion about how to live as a Christian is an indication of a spirit of error. Saints who have been around the church for many years should not begin questioning their God-given life-style standards. The way that Christians live is an element understood early on. This confusion comes from questions the devil suggests. He loves to contend God's standards are no longer necessary or there is something God is trying to keep us from. Do not forget, Satan is a liar and he wants to make you just like him – full of rebellion.

Apple trees bare apples and leaders produce in others what they are. Those who are under the influence of one not preaching the truth generate followers of false doctrine. Jesus made it simple to understand.

Most of the time, these followers are more impressed with the false prophet than with Jesus Christ. They become disciples of the false preacher instead of Jesus.

Another mark of a false prophet is the overall disrespect they have for those under their care. They are not looking out for the care of others, but looking out for their own interests and how they appear to their community. They want to make sure they are seen in a "good light" and that they appear perfect in their presentation. These are leaders producing corrupt fruit. Beware of this type of leadership that produces performers instead of disciples of Jesus Christ.

Chapter 10
A Look at Romans 16:17,18

"Now I beseech you, brethren, mark them which cause
divisions and offences contrary to the doctrine which
ye have learned; and avoid them. For they that are such
serve not our Lord Jesus Christ, but their own belly;
and by good words and fair speeches deceive the hearts
of the simple" (Romans 16:17,18).

Paul warned the Roman church to beware of those who
cause divisions opposing the doctrine already learned. We must
apply this warning to ourselves also.

The divisions Paul is addressing here is about those who divide the church by using false doctrines (teachings). False teachers want *controlled* division in a congregation as they introduce
their false teachings.

This may sound unthinkable, but it serves a purpose for developing deception. The more converts to their way of thinking
creates more pressure against those who are upholding truth.

When a false prophet begins their journey into error they
often cause divided opinions in the people because of their
wandering between two opinions. If a false prophet changed

everything immediately, the resistance would be nearly impossible to overcome. The plan is to divide and then conquer in smaller groups. They find the individuals of influence and begin training them to sway members in their circle of friends. Over time, all of the smaller units will begin to unite under the banner of false doctrine.

Not every one under the false prophet's tutelage is deceived and will naturally resist. Since resisting leadership is rebellious, this leaves the saint in a bad position. Their resistance can be with the wrong attitude and by doing so they step into one of the devil's traps.

Bitterness can engross their lives and turn them into a critic of everything that is done. Now you have two problems, false doctrine in the leader and a bad attitude in the laity. Both are wrong and are doomed for the judgment of God. Still, God can show the way for healing in both conditions if they will fall on the Rock, be broken, and repent.

This is where we must stop and remember who the Head of the church is. Jesus will not allow His body to be overcome by false prophets and their doctrines. This does not mean that whole churches or religious organizations cannot fall prey to false doctrine and go into apostasy. This has happened many times over nearly 2000 years of Christianity. What it does mean, however, is those who fall away are not Jesus Christ's church anyway, so we can remain confident. God will still have a church in the end that loves His truth; we must be determined to be in it.

The church will have to repeatedly overcome false prophets. We must overcome "winds" of false doctrine every day in our families and churches to be saved. We are not going to the Holy City without the "good fight of faith."

It is not the will of God for His church to fall into false doctrine. Those in the laity must remember to go to the Chief Shepherd and ask for His intervention. We must go to the Head of the church. Do not be foolish to think you can confront leadership and straighten them out. This is not pleasing to God, plus it is not the saint's responsibility. Either the leader will respond to God through the prayer of the church or God will move them out. The body does not have to lift a fleshly finger. God always answers prayer that is within His will. It is the will of God for doctrinal purity. By the way, leave the timing to God, it leaves less mess.

Most serious church problems and splits are about truth against error when you get below the surface. Most only see the superficial things, like fighting about the color of carpet or how much money to spend on projects, thinking these are the causes of conflict. They are only easy issues used for taking sides. If two opposing groups develop in a church, you know you have the spirit of error present. Church divisions are the work of the devil.

The church has always had the struggle of doctrinal division, but Satan has never been successful – God will always have a church that preaches truth.

Good Word and Fair Speeches

Now let's look at "good words and fair speeches" in Romans 16:18 (refer to this chapter's opening). Fancy words and great oratory has deceived hearts of people for centuries. Great public speaking is not the hallmark of truth.

Many have tried to become better public speakers to please the people they speak to, but hidden in this desire to impress is an error that will destroy the learner.

Satan wants us to teach and preach for the immediate emotional response from the listeners so we are hooked on the "high" of hearing the roar of the crowd. He also wants us to ask around and look for compliments after we have finished our lessons or messages. He knows if he can concern us with what people think man will control us and not God.

We are not always preaching for immediate results, but a response in the lifestyle. We may never realize what affect the preached Word has until many weeks or even years later. The Word of God is seed. We plant the seed under the soil and the plant comes up as evidence of sowing. We are to plant and water – God gives the increase.

Paul also said to avoid those whose god is there belly (what is in it for them). Their fleshly appetite motivates their behavior. Those motivated by majority votes will move to the pull of carnal desires. They are always looking around at what other churches are doing to attract a crowd – what is "working" right now.

We also must remove the attitude of appearing "polished" to those who visit our churches and hear us. Brokenness in the preacher and saint will bring brokenness in the hearer just as professionalism generates more professionalism. Performance oriented churches are entertaining the spirit of error – their god is their belly (carnal desires).

Chapter 11
Try the Spirits

"Beloved, believe not every spirit, but try the spirits whether they are of God: because many false prophets are gone out into the world" (1 John 4:1)

Some people think that all false prophets are weirdoes. The devil always makes sure there is a steady stream of extreme weirdoes around so we will define false prophets by them.

Many say, "Oh, that weirdo is a false prophet, anyone can tell that." What they fail to realize is false prophets do not appear weird to everyone. Most are normal acting and defended by people who love them. Don't forget, Jesus said they would be wolves dressed up like harmless lambs.

False prophets are usually trying to convince you that they are harmless and that you should like them. Convincing you of their authenticity is their goal. In addition, they often assert they do not want to hurt anybody.

We must "try the spirits whether they are of God." When we try the spirits, we are making them prove they are of God. There is a test to show if we are entertaining a real or false prophet.

The Test

> "Though I speak with the tongues of men and of angels, and have not charity, I am become *as* sounding brass, or a tinkling cymbal. And though I have *the gift of* prophecy, and understand all mysteries, and all knowledge; and though I have all faith, so that I could remove mountains, and have not charity, I am nothing. And though I bestow all my goods to feed *the poor*, and though I give my body to be burned, and have not charity, it profiteth me nothing" (1 Corinthians 13:1-3).

God loves people, but does the prophet? Love is the greatest test, because God is Love. Does the prophet love himself more than the truth?

God revealed Himself in the body of a man. His name was Jesus. He gave himself as a sacrifice for the sins of humanity. He was not self-serving; He "spent" Himself throughout His ministry, and then, ultimately with His life. When He was tested, He revealed what Spirit controlled Him by doing the will of God – not the desires of the flesh.

All prophets when tested will reveal what spirit controls them. This then is the key of understanding – know the spirit that controls the prophet.

The Apostle John said, "Many false prophets are gone out into the world." This is why we cannot believe a person just because he is holding the Bible when he speaks. Many false brothers are with the true church and are not revealed because we have not tested what spirit they are of.

> If there arise among you a prophet, or a dreamer of dreams, and giveth thee a sign or a wonder, And the sign or the wonder come to pass, whereof he spake unto thee, saying, Let us go after other gods, which thou hast not known, and let us serve them; Thou shalt not hearken unto the words of that prophet, or that dreamer of dreams: for the LORD your God proveth you, to know whether ye love the LORD your God

with all your heart and with all your soul. (Deuteronomy 13:1-3)

Here is another test. God wants to know who it is that loves His precepts. He will find out by allowing false prophets to exist among us. He will find out who loves truth by who protects it. We all protect that which gives us security and power. Therefore, what you see the prophet protecting is his god.

These verses in Deuteronomy 13 were instructions to the children of Israel. In the last days of the church age, we would do well to heed this same warning. There will be an increase in the showing of signs and wonders by false prophets to make us think they are prophets of God. We must ask ourselves the *purpose* of the sign or wonder; is it to attract our attention to follow an individual or cause us to seek after the gods of this world? Is it to promote idolatry?

God has designed this test to reveal our resolve and defense of the true message. If the sign or wonder appeals to your flesh making you believe in a different gospel, you have a false prophet on your hands.

God has always used miraculous signs and wonders to show He operates beyond man's ability. Satan is a copycat of God and has wanted to be like God from the beginning. He will use signs and wonders by his prophets to get you to believe in his false ways.

The key of understanding is looking at the purpose of the sign or wonder; does it give glory to Almighty God or to man? Does it promote a cause other than people being born again and following through in spiritual maturity? Does it promote the unity in the church?

It is time to throw away the devil's junk and see the true manifestation of the Spirit of God. He is a miracle working God, but the glory belongs to Him alone. We must forsake sensationalism promoting men and programs above God and His power. When man gets the credit, you can be sure what spirit controls the prophet.

Once people start on the road of impressing others, they never find the end of their appetite for man's approval. They will have to build it better, sing it better, promote it with greater fanfare, convince and convince again that they really have it to-gether and their church is the most comfortable place in town. There will be programs for every subgroup pushing for more and more attention to their specialized issues.

The carnal wants of people is not what moves Jesus. It is faith in His Word, provision, and power. He is looking for our confidence in His purpose for our lives, not our purpose for Him.

"Preach the word; be instant in season, out of season; reprove, rebuke, exhort with all longsuffering and doc-trine. For the time will come when they will not endure sound doctrine; but after their own lusts shall they heap to themselves teachers, having itching ears; And they shall turn away their ears from the truth, and shall be turned unto fables" (2 Timothy 4:2-4).

It has always been the first priority to preach truth to those who hear us. Paul told Timothy some people would not endure sound doctrine. People have not changed. Many today do not persist in true doctrine. They allow every wind of doctrine to en-tice them with what appeals to their fleshly desires.

Paul said the time would come when the lusts of people would determine whom they trusted for truth. However, none of us can trust the flesh to detect truth. If someone is appealing to us by using what pleases the flesh, we have a fraud. This is why we must rebuke this spirit and insist on the original revelation of apostolic doctrine.

Second Peter Chapter Two

This chapter gives insight into the workings of false prophets and teachers. Peter gives some strong words to be heeded.

If Peter recognized false prophets in the early church, then they are surely with us right now, in hiding, waiting for opportunities to introduce destructive heriesies. It will never be an "in your face" approach, but a sneaking in of thoughts into the minds of the people. They are cunning people that know how to change people's ideas over time.

In addition, if you see people grouping together in liberal or conservitive groups you have herisy. This is not God's will for the church body. God does not have political parties. There is only one Head; Jesus Christ. All information comes from One Spirit. If there is disunity, you have more than one influencing spirit.

Paul told the church at Ephesus, "There is one body, and one Spirit, even as ye are called in one hope of your calling; One Lord, one faith, one baptism, One God and Father of all, who is above all, and through all, and in you all" (Ephesians 4:4-6).

In Second Peter, the Apostle goes on to say, the true message will become tarnished by immoral actions. The immorality may be covered for a time, but when revealed it will injure the reputation of the church because the false prophet claims to be of God. Many people walk away from truth never to return because of this. The false prophet will be held responsible by God for misrepresenting Him.

This is why we must teach trust in Jesus Christ and not in man, because they can fail. Those in step with the Spirit are the true leaders – follow them as long as they continue in the faith.

The greed of false workers will take advantage of people with lies and cunning advice. People will give almost everything they have and follow deceptive practices housed in charisma and a good time.

God has judged the ways of false teaching and preaching. Beware, it will come down. When the church perceives error in her midst, she is responsible to pull it down by authority in the name of Jesus Christ. When the church activates against error, false doctrine and teachers are revealed.

False prophets scoff at those who preach the truth. Scoffers are mockers. They will always belittle holders to the original teachings of the Apostles. They chide them for being locked in the past. But the original gospel message is timeless. It is universal. We cannot change it to meet the demands of a world wanting to manage sin.

"For such are false apostles, deceitful workers, trans-forming themselves into the apostles of Christ. And no marvel; for Satan himself is transformed into an angel of light. Therefore it is no great thing if his ministers also be transformed as the ministers of righteousness; whose end shall be according to their works" (2 Corinthians 11:13-15).

Part 4
What Shall We Do?

Chapter 12
Living by the New Standard

Since God has settled what sin is, don't think we can start a debate and get a different answer. God gave Moses the Law to define sin. No matter how loud we protest we are not going to change His mind. Yet, God did make a huge change in who takes the penalty for sins. In addition, He introduced a way to identify sin before it ever becomes an act. This new way of living begins with a new birth. We must be born again to enter and see this new kingdom (see John 3).

> "But this *shall be* the covenant that I will make with the house of Israel; After those days, saith the LORD, I will put my law in their inward parts, and write it in their hearts; and will be their God, and they shall be my people" (Jeremiah 31:33).

The Holy Ghost blew into the upper room, as recorded in Acts chapter two, and filled those who were waiting for the promise of the Father, fulfilling this prophecy of Jeremiah along with other Old Testament prophecies.

All who are born again do so by hearing the written Word of

God preached, which in turn brings faith in Jesus Christ. This faith brings obedience to water baptism in Jesus' name and the infilling of the Holy Ghost. It will not be a sermon from the mind and will of man that saves our souls. The Apostle Paul told the Corinthian church, "For after that in the wisdom of God the world by wisdom knew not God, it pleased God by the <u>foolishness of preaching to save</u> them that believe" (1 Corinthians 1:21 [underscoring by author]).

Obedience to the leading of the Holy Ghost inside of the believer never breaks the law of God. There is no penalty for doing right. This new covenant of the Holy Ghost is better because it leads us to do the right things and away from doing wrong. The Holy Ghost is a holiness teacher.

When anyone receives the Holy Ghost, God places in the mind and heart the New Covenant that is stricter than the Mosaic Law is. This new Law is an *internal* guidance system that reveals sin before it becomes an action and then a lifestyle.

The key for Adam and Eve's eternal life was to obey the Word of God. The key for the Holy Ghost filled person is the same; we must obey God's Word through the new covenant of the Holy Ghost. The Holy Ghost does not do away with the written Word of God; it validates and confirms what the Spirit is teaching us. If obeyed, the Holy Ghost fulfills the intent of the Law of God, which is righteousness.

In Matthew chapter five, Jesus explained how the Old Law given to Moses was a set of standards the children of Israel were to live by. Jesus then introduced His new standard by saying several times, "But I say unto you," after quoting one of the Old Commandments. In essence, He was telling His believers that He was introducing something new for them.

The Law given on Mount Sinai defined sin. It shows that all people, including those in our era, are also sinners. The Law of Moses is a curse because it proves everyone is a sinner, dooming us to death. Nevertheless, Jesus instituted what he called a fulfilling or satisfying of the Law by His life's work. This was a brand new thing and it extinguished the doom. He said, "Think not that I am come to destroy the law, or the prophets: I am not come to destroy, but to fulfil" (Matthew 5:17).

Jesus lived His life without sinning. Therefore, the Law did not define who He was. Instead, He defined true righteousness — He fulfilled the Law. No one had ever lived a sinless life until He was born into this world. He has shown true righteousness, which has no law against it. His life was Holy.

If Jesus had destroyed the law, as false teachings have implied, He would have removed the rules or standards proving man a sinner. Instead, He fulfilled the righteousness required by the Law *and* paid the penalty for sin. His righteousness came by having the mind of God that produces actions without sin. This made Him the perfect sacrifice and perfect example for us.

He then made all of the old tabernacle/temple practices obsolete. Here are some of the things Jesus did for us:

- Became sin for us through His death.
- Became the sacrifice for our sins – the spotless sacrificial Lamb.
- Became the only holy (separate from sin) High Priest to administer the atonement for the sins of all people of all time.
- Paid the price for our sins even though He was not guilty of any sin himself.

God is Holy. Holiness does not have sin in it. There is no place in God where you will find sin because He is Holy. His holy mind produced a holy life in Jesus Christ, and it still does in those who obey.

Those who receive the Holy Ghost (Acts 2) now have the power to identify sin before it becomes an action and then a lifestyle. We could call it Jesus' Rule, and it is the highest standard known to man. Jesus wanted to move away from only using a written external standard to identify sin after it was committed. Thus, He instituted a standard to stop the cause of sin in the mind and heart.

The Old Testament Law said, "thou shalt not kill," but Jesus said, "…That whosoever is angry with his brother without a cause shall be in danger of the judgment:"

To Jesus, the development of the attitude and identifying the motivation was where the standard should be set. One can say, "don't kill," but to be able to enforce this law you must have a corpse, killer, and a witness. Jesus' Rule stops murder before it ever becomes an act. Jesus defined the *cause* of murder in the mind or heart as sin. Hatred has become murder under this new standard. We can see then, that Jesus' Rule is stricter than the Law of Moses. It judges sin before it becomes an action, but you have to be the judge of yourself.

Jesus knew that just judging a person as a murderer did not save him from being a sinner. However, if He could give him a method of never developing the attitude of a murder, He could stop the act of murder. Jesus' Rule sets us free from the cause of sin so it will no longer master us. No wonder Jesus said, "If the Son therefore shall make you free, ye shall be free indeed."

Jesus' Law is the most powerful law in existence. His Law of the Spirit requires us to eliminate the causes of sin. This is why we must practice and teach good listening skills when God speaks to us. The Holy Ghost will speak to us about every aspect of our lives if we have an ear to hear.

It was against the Law of Moses to do what a commandment said not to do, while for Jesus' Rule it is against His Law to allow conception of sin (defined by the written Word) in our hearts. Conception is the coming together of temptation and human lust. Together, they are a deadly combination. This is why Paul taught us to mortify (kill) the deeds of the body. The desires of the flesh must not dominate our lives. The "old man" of sinning flesh must be "buried" to never live again. The first chapter of the book of James also deals with this subject,

> "Let no man say when he is tempted, I am tempted of God: for God cannot be tempted with evil, neither tempteth he any man: But every man is tempted, when he is drawn away of his own lust, and enticed. Then when lust hath conceived, it bringeth forth sin: and sin, when it is finished, bringeth forth death" (James 1:13-15).

Once again, looking at Jesus' Rule from Matthew chapter five, we see he also spoke of adultery as being a part of the Law of Moses. A sexual relationship outside of marriage had to have already happened to break the Law of "thou shalt not commit adultery." Jesus' Standard or Rule arrests the look and the thought of lust before it becomes a sinful action. This is the Royal Law of Christ of loving others, as we love ourselves. Love does not take another person's spouse or sin against their own spouse because Love treats others, as we would like to be treated.

> "If ye fulfil the royal law according to the scripture, Thou shalt love thy neighbour as thyself, ye do well…" (James 2:8).

Allowing the Holy Ghost to guide our lives is to live in the Love of God. Paul told the Roman church, "The love of God is shed abroad in our hearts by the Holy Ghost which is given unto us" (Romans 5:5). Shed abroad means to "gush" into those filled with the Holy Ghost. God's Love does not just trickle into us; it gushes into the believers who allow the flow of Love to be channeled through their lives. We are not a container but a conduit of God's Spirit.

Another important standard set by Jesus was not returning evil for evil, but to overcome evil with good. We must learn to absorb wrong, by the grace of God, to bring victory over evil. This is the opposite of what our flesh would do, but those who are Christ-like are dead to the fleshly demand of fighting for their own rights.

> "Ye have heard that it hath been said, An eye for an eye, and a tooth for a tooth: But I say unto you, That ye resist not evil: but whosoever shall smite thee on thy right cheek, turn to him the other also. And if any man will sue thee at the law, and take away thy coat, let him have *thy* cloak also. And whosoever shall compel thee to go a mile, go with him twain" (Matthew 5:38-41).

Christians do not "get even" with someone for the evil they have done. This attitude of not returning evil for evil is rare in a world full of guns, knives, lawyers, litigation, little league fights and barroom brawls. The idea of overcoming evil with good is a godly standard that will change any family, society or church into a society of peace. People of any group desiring to "get even" for any evil done will produce strife, friction, and confusion. Only the wise have peace.

In Conclusion

Under God's plan, all sin must have a sacrifice as payment. Jesus Christ became the single sacrifice for all sin. This included past, present, and future sins committed by the human race. Since Jesus took the penalty for sin, we can charge our personal sins to Jesus Christ, our sacrificial Lamb, and never pick them up again. This is the purpose for the name of Jesus Christ in water baptism – to literally remove the sins and the penalty of sin from our lives, which is death. Jesus died so we would not have to. He lives so we may live eternally through obedience to the Word of God. The baptism of the Holy Ghost is the law of God written on our hearts. If we listen to the Spirit, we will not fulfill the lust of the flesh.

Once again consider the Word of God, "For if that first *covenant* had been faultless, then should no place have been sought for the second. For finding fault with them, he saith, Behold, the days come, saith the Lord, when I will make a new covenant with the house of Israel and with the house of Judah: Not according to the covenant that I made with their fathers in the day when I took them by the hand to lead them out of the land of Egypt; because they continued not in my covenant, and I regarded them not, saith the Lord. For this *is* the covenant that I will make with the house of Israel after those days, saith the Lord; I will put my laws into their mind, and write them in their hearts: and I will be to them a God, and they shall be to me a people: And they shall not teach every man his neighbour, and every man his brother, saying, Know the Lord: for all shall know me, from the least to the greatest. For I will be merciful to their unrighteousness, and their sins and their iniquities will I remember no more" (Hebrews 8:7-12).

Chapter 13
God's Power or Man's Power?

"And I, brethren, when I came to you, came not with
excellency of speech or of wisdom, declaring unto you
the testimony of God" (1 Corinthians 2:1).

Paul approached his ministry to the church with meekness
and fear becaused he realized how dangerous his flesh was. If he
allowed his flesh to become "alive," he would follow his fleshly
desires. He knew how to crusify the flesh with its affections and
lust. We must also, or we will become monsters instead of
ministers.

It is time for us to stop putting our trust in what humans can
do. Since the beginning of mankind we have seen great
advancements and achievements. But, man will never advance
beyond God. No matter how great our acheivements are, we still
have to trust in the power of God. God is the Creator and we are
the created.

No man-made invention has outdone the power of the Holy
Ghost living inside of a person. No author has reached the level
of power within the written Word of God. No psychologist has
penetrated the soul like the Word of God can. And, no bank

account is big enough to buy the Kingdom of God.

It is time to stop waiting for mammon (materialism) to do the will of God. We hear from God to do many things, but stop short when we think we do not have the means to do it. God will never tell us to go without the resources to do so. We may not see the resources, but they are there, ready to be released at the right time. God is looking for Abram-like obedience.

The Kingdom of God is not just about construction of physical buildings. It's about building people fitly framed together as the church (Ephesians 2:20,21). God will always provide what we need to do His work. If God directs us to do something for Him, move on it and do it, the money will be there, the strength will be there, the words will come – every resource will be supplied. Remember, the just shall *live by* faith, not talk by faith or think by faith. We must start living by faith. Yes, *living* by faith.

Have we done so well living by our own power that we no longer need an Almighty God to work miracles? Do we really need His power any longer to achieve what we need or can we accomplish it by ourselves?

As we look at our church gatherings each week, are they void of the miraculous. Are we singing to entertain ourselves or singing praise from hearts of worship to God? Is our teaching and preaching mere oritory or has He spoken directly to His people through His servants? Do we show up to get "filled in" from the "grapevine," or are we plugged into the True Vine, producing the fruit of the Spirit?

We must have more than human effort in our gatherings, otherwise we will become one of the many denominations made by the hands of men. They have no value in the Kingdom of God.

Competiton vs. Cooperation

Our lives are either built on competition or cooperation. Satan promotes competition while Jesus Christ developments cooperation. This is how to tell which is the true church. Those who have a competitive spirit are always looking to out-promote the other churches in town with new gimmicks each week. It is obvious observing the amount of copy-cat programs from one denomination to the next. Copying man-made ideas is a dead end.

Competition is about being better than the other guy. To be better than the other party makes someone the looser. This has been a trap from the devil to plunge us into envy with one another. Competitive local churches watch other churches suffer when there may be no need for them to suffer at all. They may be in need of prayer to help them break through evil spirits in there city, but the "better" church just sits back and blames that church for being spiritually weak.

There may be a financial need that could be taken care of quickly and painlessly by a neighboring church, but that may make the receipiant appear more "successful." Competitive spirits do not work in the Kingdom of God – they are damaging and distructive.

Cooperation is something very different. Cooperation is about being a servant to Jesus Christ and His body of believers. Jesus told us, the greatest in the Kingdom are those who are servants to all. It's not about being better than someone else, but about making the whole body better by our service to one another.

Competition is about comparison to one another while cooperation is about comparison to the standard set by Jesus Christ, which is love. He was a servant to all. He never promoted the idea of being better than, but promoted childlike humility creating an attitude of a servant.

We must learn that greatness is not promoting ourselves above others – it's helping others become greater for the good of the whole body.

Chapter 14
Unify or Die

Church unity is a deception buster. People, who think they can live for God by themselves, move toward false ways. God designed His body to work in unity, preventing the spirit of error from creeping in. Churches that develop schisms are in the greatest danger of false doctrine coming in.

Love confronts every false way. We need to learn about the true Love of God that confronts for the good of the Body. It heals schisms and old hurts. To be Christian is to work out all of our differences. There really is no choice – we must live together in unity. Even if we have to stay up all night to bring unity, it is worth it. If we do not struggle for it, we are identifying ourselves with the spirit of error. The way of error is refusing to heal broken fellowship.

One blemish of our times is the attitude of making the other party responsible to resolve ill feelings and old hurts. Waiting for the other party to start may cancel it from ever happening.

A true Christian never holds grudges for years from the offences of the past. Members of the Body of Christ must work out all difference quickly. Holding grudges and seeking vengeance reveals the spirit of error. Grudges and vengeance is the substance of Satan's kingdom. To be right in the sight of God is to build on His foundation He used for building the church – forgiveness.

"And when ye stand praying, forgive, if ye have ought against any: that your Father also which is in heaven may forgive you your trespasses. But if ye do not forgive, neither will your Father which is in heaven forgive your trespasses" (Mark 11:25,26).

John told us to walk in the Light. In the Light, there is fellowship with Jesus and with one another. If we say, we are in the Light and hate our brother, we have lied – the truth is not in us. Fellowship in the Light reveals truth among us. To be out of fellowship with a brother or sister is sin because unforgiving attitudes locks us out of God's forgiveness.

Fellowship is what brings the covering of the blood of Jesus on our lives. The blood only covers the fellowship existing in Jesus Christ, not factions that have broken away.

If we do not unify, a one world religious system is positioning itself and will entice our churches into a "thriving" organism that is doing it "exactly right." It is the false way of ecumenicalism and ultimately interfaith practices. The interfaith movement is sweeping our world now by bringing together all religious beliefs, not just the branches of "Christianity."

Spiritual Warfare

Spiritual warfare continually removes all things not of God from the church. Many have thought spiritual warfare is dancing around the church building shouting and singing things at the devil to scare him away. This works about as well as a rain dance.

There have even been those who also claim just praising God in a church building will drive away the devil. It is true that God does dwell in the praises of His people, however, we should not "play around" with the devil daily and then attempt to run him off during church services. Eventually we will become fake worshippers and our praise will not accomplish anything more than fooling those who are carnally minded.

True worshippers of God are those totally given to His purpose. There is overcoming power in this kind of believer. The true believer is committed to the leading of the Holy Ghost. They wear the proper war armor of the Lord and are the only ones who can fight spiritual warfare.

> "Stand therefore, having your loins girt about with truth, and having on the breastplate of righteousness; And your feet shod with the preparation of the gospel of peace; Above all, taking the shield of faith, wherewith ye shall be able to quench all the fiery darts of the wicked. And take the helmet of salvation, and the sword of the Spirit, which is the word of God: Praying always with all prayer and supplication in the Spirit, and watching thereunto with all perseverance and supplication for all saints" (Ephesians 6:14-18).

These verses show us seven things Satan would love to steal from the church. They are *truth, righteousness, the gospel, faith, salvation, the Word of God,* and *prayer.* If he can remove them, we will not be able to fight against His deception. The whole armor of God gives us defense against the Master Deceiver. Without the armor, we only have the flesh. Those who live by the flesh cannot please God and certainly cannot defeat deception.

The first of the seven is *truth.* God must reveal it, because it is His truth. Therefore, it is Satan's plan to bring deception to hide that truth revealed to the believers or to steal the Word before it can take root in our hearts. Satan's lies pervert what God has revealed to His church.

The second is *righteousness,* which is living by Jesus' Rule or Standard. Righteousness is not automatic for the human race. Obedience to the leading of the Holy Ghost generates living right. If Satan can replace Jesus' standards with his own, we will become slaves to sin once again.

The death, burial, and resurrection of Jesus Christ has brought to humanity the "good news" that we can be liberated from the bondage of sin. This is the third piece Satan desires to steal – *the gospel* message of the church. Satan wants us to change the message so individuals will remain enslaved to him. He does not care what you believe as long as you do not find the message of freedom from the bondage of a sinful life.

As for the fourth piece of armor, Satan wants to destroy the church's *faith* (confidence) in God by introducing lies causing unbelief. Satan twists God's testing of His people into a belief that God does not care about us. We must not loose faith when we are tested. The trial of our faith is precious because it produces a greater faith in God, not destruction.

The fifth is *salvation* The name of Jesus means, salvation from sin. He came to save the world from lives of sin. The name of Jesus is important because it obtains the true meaning of repentance – stop sinning and turn to the Savior for deliverance. The name also contains power over sin for us when baptized in water using the name of Jesus Christ. There is no other name given to mankind bringing salvation (Acts 4:12).

The Word of God will reign forever. This is the sixth item – *the Word* – it will judge every person. This is why Satan has a grand design of making the Word of God seem like restrictions against what we should have. He wants us to feel God is withholding pleasant things from us.

Finally, there is *prayer*. Satan teaches self-sufficiency so we will abandon communications with Jesus Christ. To pray is to admit our need of God for cleansing and godly direction. The devil wants to destroy a good relationship between God and man, so he hates prayer. He also hates intercessory prayer warriors. If he can, he will stop them.

These elements of spiritual armor are necessary for survival against the cunning of Satan. If we do not keep these pieces securely on, we will be defeated – definitely.

* * * *

Remember, helping people who are in deception can be bothersome if you look at it selfishly. It takes the wisdom of God and great courage to challenge thinking that is wrong, especially when they feel they are right. It also places us in a vulnerable position in our own walk with God.

"If a man be overtaken in a fault, ye which are spiritual, re-store such an one in the spirit of meekness; considering thyself, lest thou also be tempted," Paul said in Galatians chapter six and verse one. Be warned, fighting false doctrine can pull you in. There is a danger of becoming what we fight. This is why we must always work in the fellowship of Jesus Christ to remain in the truth.

The idea of being the only one to fight this insidious monster is also a deception. Other members of the body will work with you – don't do it alone. Hesitation to ask for help will bring deception and eventual destruction to you also.

> "For though we walk in the flesh, we do not war after the flesh: (For the weapons of our warfare *are* not carnal, but mighty through God to the pulling down of strong holds;) Casting down imaginations, and every high thing that exalteth itself against the knowledge of God, and bringing into captivity every thought to the obedience of Christ" (2 Corinthians 10:3-5).

Conquerors or Conquered?

We either are conquerors or conquered. There is no middle ground in the church. Everyone's spiritual eyes and ears must be alert to the possibility of Satan's deceptions. To pretend there is no struggle against winds of doctrine indicates spiritual apathy. Death waits nearby.

The Apostle John wrote in his book, The Revelation of Jesus Christ, to the seven churches in Asia (Revelation 2 and 3). The true gospel message was the foundation of these churches. Nevertheless, spirits of error had crept into their attitudes and actions. John was deliberate in his warnings to these churches – change your ways or face removal from the body of Christ.

Each church had things that were right. Nevertheless, God was not willing to let the things that were wrong linger without a warning. Even today, the Spirit of God is speaking a warning to us. We are doing some things right, but at the same time many of us are allowing the spirit of error to weave itself into the fabric of our lifestyles.

John repeatedly wrote the words, "He that hath an ear, let him hear what the Spirit saith unto the churches." The "ear" is for spiritual hearing – to give undivided attention to the voice of the Lord. This is the only way for the church to know if we have an internal problem needing correction. The Spirit of God will always warn us of our error.

God gave each of the seven churches the same instruction, "He that overcometh…" The Spirit warned them not to be complacent with their state of affairs. Most had more than one thing to overcome. Yes, they had to work together to uproot and destroy those things that were false among them.

If we, today, have "settled in" and think we are okay the way we are, we are spiritually deaf. God is speaking to us now about those things that will destroy us if we do not *overcome* them. The church is an overcoming body. It will be a daily challenge until Jesus comes for His bride. The bride of Jesus Christ is together in doctrine and practice.

For additional copies of this book,
please write to:

Timothy Duffy
3762 West Old 30, Lot 55E
Warsaw, IN 46580
Or visit our website: http://members.kconline.com/dot

Please enclose $5.00 per book
(this includes postage and packaging)
Make checks or money orders payable to Tim Duffy.